How the Establishment Rigged the Electoral System

(And got away with it)

Thomas Conner

PREFACE

In the general election of 2015, 22 million votes cast by British voters were effectively thrown in the bin. It was three-quarters of those who voted. These votes are euphemistically known as "wasted votes". The voters need not have bothered showing up at the polling station. Mainstream news channels, in so far as one observed, the BBC, ITN, and Sky, passed not a single comment on this scandal, but then they are part of the establishment propaganda machine so why would they? The Labour and Conservative party leadership in Parliament consider it a price worth paying if it keeps them in power, and it has done. For almost a century. Paradoxically, three quarters of the members of the Labour Party support electoral reform. As for members of the Conservative Party, not so many. In this book, I do my best to expose the base and offensive political morality of the leaderships of the Labour and Conservative Parties, and how the fraudulent electoral system they preserve protect and defend was engineered by a dishonest and corrupt establishment.

TABLE OF CONTENTS

PREAMBLE

How winning candidates are chosen in general elections in the United Kingdom has no basis in law. It is a fraud, perpetrated by the English establishment. This book will show why this is so and provide insight into the legal status of the system. Relevant case law and statutes are cited. The book will show two things. First, that the system has no legal basis at all, and second, that the system infringes the human rights of our citizens. Justification for all conclusions and assertions will be set out comprehensively.

In 2016, at the request of Prime Minister David Cameron and the Conservative Party, under pressure from the United Kingdom Independence Party and its charismatic leader Nigel Farage, those citizens of the United Kingdom entitled to vote in referendums were asked to say whether they wished their country to continue as a member of the European Union or to leave the bloc. 52% of the people who voted (17.4 million) voted to leave. Supporters of the leave campaign, politicians, and journalists, stressed on the media and television how critical it was that the wishes of the 17.4 million should not be thwarted lest our democracy be called into question. It was a flood of commentary.

In 2015, just one year earlier, the votes of the 17.4 million were preceded in the general election of that year by the votes of 22 million UK citizens that were discarded to the waste bin and ignored. These votes are euphemistically referred to as "wasted" votes. Not one politician or journalist called out this scandal. Yes indeed, three quarters of the votes of those who voted in the general election of 2015 were discarded to the waste bin and ignored. Scandalous facts such as these while not necessarily hidden from the public tend to go unreported by the BBC, ITN, and Sky News. On election night TV coverage, it would not be difficult for the broadcasters to report wasted vote quantities by constituency alongside the results. A running total could be kept and reported as an election outcome. In this way, the broadcasters would be the catalysts of a new dialogue with the public. Unfortunately, they simply report the results but contribute nothing. The failure of Sky News, the BBC News, and ITN News, to comment on such a scandal does rather tend to suggest that their journalists can go so far but no further. When push comes to shove, these channels are controlled by the government propaganda machine. Correction, the establishment propaganda machine. Even the bravest journalists have mortgages to pay.

The United Kingdom is a Constitutional Monarchy. It is not a democracy and never has been. Universal suffrage is not democracy. How could it be when so many votes are wasted and do not contribute to the composition of the legislature?

Representative systems of voting are essential attributes in a truly democratic state, but of course "democracy" is characterised by much more than electoral systems. Central to the notion are the rule of law, the peaceful transition of power, a free press, and other freedoms such as freedom of association and speech, and the right *to petition the government for a redress of grievances* (this last part borrowed from the first amendment to the US Constitution). Many commentators ascribe the arrival of "democracy" in the United Kingdom to the 1928 legislation which gave women the vote on the same terms as men thus ushering in universal adult suffrage. As already stated, universal suffrage is not "Democracy", simply one of its constituent parts.

INTRODUCTION

This is not the story of or history of the system of voting used in British general elections, although some of that story is told. Rather, it is a tale of two events of immense historical significance that determined how the outcomes of general elections in the late nineteenth century, the twentieth century, and beyond, would be arrived at. One is the result of an error or omission by Civil Service lawyers in 1872, and the other is the result of a deliberate act of malfeasance by Royal Commissioners in 1910.

It is also a story about human rights, and how the implications and effects of the human right to vote have been undermined by successive British Governments and indeed by the judges of the European Court of Human Rights in Strasbourg.

The First Event

The first event was in the nineteenth century, that hundred years that began with what is usually called the Unreformed Parliament, at a time of considerable electoral corruption, and ended with a battle royal to achieve universal suffrage, which eventually came twenty-eight years after the century had ended and lots of women (and men) knew what a policeman's baton felt like when it struck the back of the head. The event in question was the passing of an *Act to Amend the Law Relating to Procedure at Parliamentary and Municipal Elections*, commonly known as the Ballot Act, in 1872. This act of Parliament introduced a procedure for voting in secret at general elections, prior to which voting was done in public, and corruption and intimidation and indeed mob violence and drunkenness were not uncommon on election days. In drafting the Ballot Act, the lawyers of the Civil Service left history with something of a conundrum.

The Second Event

The second event occurred in 1910 and was an attempt to solve the conundrum but with an unlawful strategy. Victorian Britain for the most part was a two-party state consisting of Liberals and Conservatives (Liberals evolved from the Whigs, and Conservatives evolved from the Tories). As the century drew to a close, several socialist(ic) groups were formed with the objective of representing the still not fully enfranchised "working class". Out of this came the Labour Party. The two-party state was now a three-party state, and a Royal Commission was established in 1908 to look at systems of voting in order to cope with the new political landscape. When they wrote their report in 1910, the Royal Commissioners went too far (i.e., included text that was ultra vires).

The Accusation - Internal

So, what exactly was it that the Royal Commissioners did that was "ultra vires"? It will be shown that the authors of the royal commission report into systems of election in 1910 tried to usurp, and did usurp, the role of the judges in the legal process of Statutory Interpretation (REPORT of the ROYAL COMMISSION appointed to enquire into ELECTORAL SYSTEMS with APPENDICES CD 5163). A royal commission may make recommendations, but it is for Parliament and the Courts to make law, and Statutory Interpretation involves formal legal rules that are exclusively applied by the Judiciary. No other person or persons may do this.

The drafting of statute law is a difficult process usually performed by Civil Service lawyers. Texts in the statutes are invariably complex and while the lawyers do their best to get it right inevitably some law is passed that is sub-optimal in meaning and so the judges have to fill the gaps. In interpreting statute law, where there are ambiguities or lacunae (gaps), the judges try to find what was the intention of Parliament. In so doing, they interpret the law. In 1910, the authors of the royal commission report into systems of election published without lawful authority a deliberately arbitrary interpretation of a Parliamentary Statute. The arbitrary interpretation went unchallenged.

The royal commission was established in 1908 to enquire into electoral systems because the hitherto binary two-party system of Liberals and Conservatives had been supplanted by the creation in 1900 of the Labour Representation Committee which in 1906 became the Labour Party, representing the interests of the "working class" (And this new party won 29 seats in the 1906 general election).

In this new political landscape, which the establishment viewed as a threat, if in three-way contests the progressive vote is split between the Liberal Party and the Labour Party then greater is the probability of the Conservative Party winning elections, which is what the Establishment wanted. If a first past-the-post system of voting using "relative majority" could be established de facto and go unchallenged, aspirations of democracy could be thwarted, which is also what the establishment wanted. The authors of the report obliged. Referring to the fourth Parliamentary Reform Act of 1918, arguably the "greatest of the series", Professor Martin Pugh reinforces this point: "the achievement in 1918 of a democratic franchise in combination with an unreformed electoral system proved to be the most significant decision of the war, for it produced a Conservative hegemony in British Government that lasted until 1945".

The Accusation - External

The European Convention on Human Rights (ECHR) contains a clause entitled Article 3 of Protocol No. 1 Right to Free Elections. This article guarantees elections at reasonable intervals by secret ballot, as well as the individual rights to vote and to stand for election. Voting is a human right, not a privilege. For fifty years, the judges in the European Court of Human Rights insisted that elections in signatory states were not required to be fair. They never said how unfair they might be, just that fair elections were not a component of human rights in this context. Wasted votes were unavoidable, they repeatedly asserted, and Article 3 of Protocol 1 did not require any of the signatory states to operate democratic systems of election to their legislative assemblies.

In 2015, however, something changed. In a case brought against the Bulgarian state, judicial thinking appeared to have been turned on its head. How this came about, and the importance of this leading case, will be shown in due course in this story.

THE BACKGROUND – WHY DOES IT MATTER?

In the general election of 1992, in the constituency of Inverness, Nairn, & Lochaber, the winning candidate Sir Russell Johnston received 13,258 votes. The second-placed candidate received 12,800 votes. The third-placed candidate received 12,562 votes. The fourth-placed candidate received 11,517 votes. The fifth-placed candidate received 766 votes. Lined up against Sir Russell Johnston's 13,258 votes were 37,645 voters who did not want him as their MP. Sir Russell Johnston packed his bags and took a flight to London to swear an oath of loyalty to Queen Elizabeth II and take his seat in the House of Commons to be the elected representative for his Highland constituency. What about the 37,645 voters who rejected him? Who would represent them?

The First Question

The first question that arises is – how is such an outcome possible? Surely this is the result of an electoral system of a banana republic or a corrupt or failed state, like Zimbabwe or The

Yemen? It is. Some banana republics and Zimbabwe and The Yemen do indeed use the same system as the United Kingdom (Of the 270 members of the Zimbabwe National Assembly, 210 are elected from single-member constituencies under first past the post).

In so far as Demos Kratia (rule by the people) gave birth to the word "Democracy", it is clear that, contrary to what the public think, the United Kingdom is not a democracy. The United Kingdom is a Constitutional Monarchy with a Parliamentary system. It is an ancient Parliamentary system with a wonderful history of evolved Parliamentary opposition to Absolute Monarchy, but it is not a Parliamentary democracy.

The Second Question

The second question that arises is – where in our Law is it written that winning candidates are chosen by Returning Officers based on this "first past the post" method? The method of selection used is usually referred to in psephology as "relative majority". It may come as something of a surprise to the public that the method of winning candidate selection by "relative majority" is not specified in our Law *anywhere*. Not in Statute Law, not in the Common Law, and not in a Statutory Instrument. It has no legal basis at all. Surprised? Then read on.

The Third Question

Obviously, this gives rise to the third question – where did the system come from, and is it legitimate? To answer this question, we shall need to look briefly at the great milestones in our electoral laws as they evolved in the nineteenth century. It is a delightful journey through (mainly) English social upheaval and gradual reform of inequality and the further gradual extension of the franchise. To illustrate the fascinating nature of the journey, let us begin with a splendid example of the terrible state of the electoral arrangements that existed in the early nineteenth century.

REFORM – A BRIEF GLANCE

The present-day English Heritage site of Old Sarum, near Salisbury, which in earlier centuries had a small population, a church and cathedral, had by the 17th century no resident voters. Eventually, it evolved into an unpopulated hillside of mud. Nevertheless, in the nineteenth century it sent two Members of Parliament to the House of Commons (including at one stage William Pitt's father Pitt the Elder) based on its eleven voters who were in fact landowners who lived elsewhere. Old Sarum was the most notorious of the "Rotten Boroughs" that were swept away by the Great Reform Act of 1832. Or, not so great reform act, depending on your point of view. Only minimal extension of the franchise was enacted, largely favouring the middle-classes over the working-class, but a system of voter registration was introduced, and rotten boroughs were abolished. A fact not widely reported outside of academic circles is that the Act disenfranchised hitherto enfranchised women. In the 18th and 17th centuries some women did qualify for the vote as property owners, but the Act for the first time linked the franchise to "Male persons" thus excluding women until 1918.

Political parties evolved throughout the century, but the dominant parties were initially the Whigs and Tories, who evolved into the Liberal Party and the Conservative Party. This evolution of the nomenclature was probably advisable, as in Gaelic tongues "Whig" meant horse-driver and "Tory" meant outlaw. Two other blocs intermittently stood for election, the Chartists seeking electoral reform such as universal suffrage, secret ballots, and payment of MPs, and the Irish Nationalists seeking independence from Britain for Ireland. The Labour Party is a creature of the twentieth century, although many political groups had been formed and were active in the late nineteenth century and it was those groups purporting to represent the "working class" who merged in 1900 to become the Labour Representation Committee. The LRC became the modern-day Labour Party in 1906.

When the small handful of obsolescent Chartist candidates and even smaller handful of independent candidates and the special case of the Irish independence parties are removed from the landscape, the political party choices available to a gradually expanding electorate, expanding thanks to the 1832 Act and later extensions of the franchise introduced by Disraeli and Gladstone, were in fact reduced to a binary choice – Whig or Tory, then later Liberal or Conservative. This can be seen from a brief summary of general election outcomes from 1832 to the milestone of Gladstone's first administration in 1868. It was during this first Gladstone administration that a definitive element of UK electoral law was written – how winning candidates in each constituency are to be selected by Returning Officers during general elections.

The first election in our examination was held shortly after the Great Reform Act of 1832. We shall then briefly summarise the elections leading up to 1868, the parties that stood, who won, and any special significance attaching to the elections and their results. When we reach the watershed election of 1852, more will be said about the Tory/Conservative and Whig/Liberal evolutions. Our brief summary will describe the outcomes of the general elections of 1832, 1835, 1837, 1841, 1847, 1852, 1857, 1859, 1865, and 1868. The leading players in our political narrative include a representative cross-section of nineteenth-century English society, such as Earl Grey, the Duke of Wellington, Viscount Melbourne, Sir Robert Peel, Lord Stanley, Lord Aberdeen, Sir John Russell, the Earl of Derby, Viscount Palmerston, Lord Beaconsfield (Benjamin Disraeli), and, lest we forget, the prole William Ewart Gladstone. (The untitled Mr. Gladstone was nonetheless a member of the upper crust of society. Of Scottish parents, but born in Liverpool, he was educated at Eton and Oxford where he gained a double first in Classics and Mathematics. Upon retiring from office after four administrations, he declined the offer of an Earldom from Queen Victoria).

BINARY BRITAIN - ELECTIONS 1832 TO 1868

The **1832** election saw the Whigs defeat the Tories where only Whig and Tory candidates stood in a binary choice.

The **1835** election saw the Whigs defeat the Conservatives where only Whig and Conservative candidates stood in a binary choice.

The **1837** election had exactly the same outcome as two years earlier, in a similar binary choice of parties.

The **1841** election was won by the Conservatives, defeating the Whigs, and where 8 Chartists stood as did an Irish home rule contingent. The choice for the Englishman was still binary.

The **1847** election was contested by the Whigs, Conservatives, one Chartist, and an Irish home rule party. Again, for the Englishman, it was a binary choice. The outcome was more nuanced, and eventually the Whigs formed a government.

The next election, in **1852**, was a watershed in British political history. The Whigs fought the Conservatives, and four Chartist candidates also stood for election. Yet still it was a binary choice for the voters. The politics were complicated, and the Conservatives ruled with difficulty for eleven months when a Whig-Radical coalition took over. It was at this time that it became clear that the Tories had evolved into the Conservative Party and represented the interests of the rural Aristocracy. The Whigs had evolved into the Liberal Party and represented the interests of the rising urban Bourgeoisie. Yet, while the term "Tory" was gradually being left behind, "Whig" was not quite dead yet.

The **1857** election saw the Whigs defeat the Conservatives in another binary choice (only one Chartist stood).

The election of **1859** was won by the Liberal Party under Lord Palmerston, defeating the Conservative Party. Only one Chartist candidate stood. Again, it was another binary choice for the voters.

The election of **1865** saw the Liberal Party under Lord Palmerston stand against only the Conservatives and win in another binary choice. This Parliament saw some highly nuanced intrigue, and a divided Liberal Party was superseded by a Conservative administration where Disraeli assumed a prominent role. This administration saw the introduction of the major electoral reform Act of 1867.

In the general election of **1868**, the Liberal Party led by W E Gladstone won a huge majority over the Conservative Party. Only three independent candidates stood. It was yet another binary choice for the electorate. During this administration, the lawyers of the Civil Service drafted a major electoral reform bill for the approval of Parliament. Under a political climate that offered repeated binary choices to the electorate – indeed since 1832 – Civil Service lawyers under the supervision of Edward Leatham the Member of Parliament for Huddersfield drafted the Ballot Act of 1872.

A major feature of electoral arrangements was that voting was done in public. This gave rise to tenants being evicted if they did not vote for the candidate of their landlord's choice, or workers losing their jobs if they did not vote as instructed by their employers (In fact, it was much worse than this. Civil unrest, intimidation, bribery, drunkenness, and violence were not uncommon on election day).

The Ballot Act introduced a procedure for secret ballots in general elections, and in so doing revolutionised British electoral law. Oddly, the Establishment was irritated as they genuinely believed that coercing the lower orders to vote how they were told to was entirely in the interests of society. Progressive thinkers however took a different view, and the legislation probably marked the start of the decline of aristocratic dominance of British electoral practise, a decline which continued throughout the remainder of the nineteenth century and into the twentieth.

NOW THE STORY REALLY BEGINS

Now, it is here that the story really begins. To tell the story, we shall jump from Gladstone in 1868 to the Edwardian era of the twentieth century and the creation of a new and potentially powerful political force called the Labour Party. First however, we shall quickly jump back again to Gladstone and the 1872 Ballot Act. The Ballot Act contained these words, quite near the beginning of the statute:

"After the close of the poll, the ballot boxes shall be sealed up so as to prevent the introduction of additional ballot papers, and shall be taken charge of by the returning officer, and that officer shall, in the presence of such agents, if any, of the candidates as may be in attendance, open the ballot boxes, and ascertain the result of the poll by counting the votes given to each candidate, and **shall forthwith declare to be elected the candidates or candidate to whom the majority of votes have been given,** *and return their names to the Clerk of the Crown in Chancery".*

These words in bold text, written into the 1872 Ballot Act, *remain to this day the law of the land* (minus the words "candidates or"). The Ballot Act had a sunset clause, and the words were transferred almost verbatim into the Representation of the People Acts (consolidated in the ROTPA 1983). The word "majority" has never been qualified with an adjective nor modified by Parliament or the Courts. The words have however, been the subject of an unlawful interpretation by the Royal Commissioners in 1910.

The words in bold text represent the first-ever occurrence of the legal rule to be followed by Returning Officers at general elections when selecting winning candidates in the constituencies. It is the *only* legal rule and has been restated with more or less identical words in subsequent iterations of the Representation of the People Acts in the twentieth century (without the words "candidates or"). As the law was drafted before 1872, when the Chartists were finished and the (Irish) Home Rule league was not founded until 1873, and as every election since 1832 left Englishmen with a binary choice, we may reasonably conclude that when the draftsmen wrote *"the candidates or candidate to whom the majority of votes have been given"* they believed that one candidate would receive more than half of the votes and the losing candidate less than half of the votes, in every constituency returning a single member. In other words, in the Ballot Act of 1872, Parliament may have been legislating that the law was that in a general election, winning candidates in single member constituencies would be chosen by *majority,* as stated in the statute, and having its usual meaning of more than half.

In Victorian England, in 1885, the Redistribution Act introduced uniform single-member constituencies across all of the United Kingdom, and with this innovation came the opportunity for the letter of the law (as specified in the Ballot Act) to be applied in future general elections.

In 1868, however, the electoral landscape was much different. In the general election of that year, while 200 constituencies did indeed elect a single member, 206 elected two members, 12 elected three members, and even one (the City of London) elected 4 members. Assuming that MPs were elected in single-member constituencies based on absolute majority (remember our binary landscape and what was written in the Ballot Act), quite clearly in all other constituencies a first past-the-post system of winning candidate selection simply would not be possible. In two-member constituencies, the system would have to be first-and-second past-the-post (ref. Conti, Parliament the Mirror of the Nation) and in constituencies returning three members by first-second-and-third past-the-post and in the City of London first-second-third-and-fourth past-the-post. What a mess. (It must be remembered that even into the 1860's it was usual practice for the Liberal and Conservative parties in two-member constituencies to nominate one candidate each. Uncontested constituencies such as these could amount to hundreds. This reality would of course have been known to the lawyers who drafted the Ballot Act. In the general election of 1859, 379 seats were uncontested, in the 1865 election 303, and in the 1868 election 212).

And so, to summarise, and to reinforce the rationale, half of the constituencies after the law was written were single-member and so members could be successfully elected according to law, by absolute majority. The other half of the constituencies returned two members but were uncontested. The Conservatives and Liberals simply put up one candidate each and no election took place. There was no need for voting. Just as there is no need for a jury to be convened where the defendant pleads guilty at the start. Quod erat demonstrandum.

What is quite clear in all of this is that it is something of a mystery why civil service lawyers specifying difficult legislation in a civil service procedure involving extensive peer review could leave a critically important word like "majority" unspecified to the extent that even a diligent search of Hansard records between 1868 and 1872 offers up no resolution to the conundrum. What can be seen from the Hansard records of the debates in the House of Commons is how hotly contested the legislation was where convictions on both sides of the debate were strongly held. What does emerge is that the Ballot Act, despite any reservations about the draftsman's failure to specify "majority" unequivocally, was widely considered to be a well-drafted piece of complex legislation. Given that it houses within its myriad of complex clauses vital elements of electoral law – how winning candidates are selected in the constituencies in a general election and a procedure for secret ballots – it behoves us to say a little more about it here.

Secret Ballots

Before the passing of the Ballot Act, voters usually stepped out from the throng to ascend a public platform full of people such as election officials, candidates, and agents. The voter would shout out their choice of candidate amidst alcohol-fuelled cheering and jeering. The voter's name and choice of candidate were noted in the polling register and the register was allowed to be published in newspapers. As the 1867 Reform Act had enfranchised thousands of workers and artisans in towns and cities, the working-class voter was in a difficult position. If a tenant, knowing his landlord was watching and from whom he had probably been given an instruction on which candidate to vote for, there was no real option. If an employee, knowing his employer was watching, the same difficulty arose. Lose your job, or lose your home, maybe both. Bribery was common, the currencies being alcohol and money, but often food too; threats by candidates were common, as were drunken brawls. Much of this malpractice vanished with the passing of the Act, but corrupt practices were still operating, particularly bribery.

The Ballot Act had to be introduced twice; the first bill passed in the House of Commons easily but was defeated in the House of Lords. Gladstone then threatened to call a general election and the Lords backed down at the second introduction. Disraeli was opposed to the measure, believing that it would "disturb and agitate the public mind". But Disraeli was not the only politician to have reservations about introducing secrecy into the way in which the British citizen exercised his right of suffrage in Victorian Britain. Gladstone himself for all of his career until he became Prime Minister was opposed to secret voting. One word that frequently arises in the rationales and speeches on the floor of the House of Commons is "manly". Advocates of retaining the practise of voting in public argued that it was the manly and open thing to do, and secrecy would taint the process, making corruption more difficult to detect.

Something had to be Done.

However, now we have to jump back to the creation of the Labour Party in 1900 – 1906. In the Edwardian era, the Establishment was not radically different from that of the late nineteenth century. In the same way that they opposed secret ballots in 1872, they opposed any notions of democracy in the early twentieth century – and for similar reasons (Gladstone himself was also opposed to notions of "democracy").

The socialist(ic) groups merged in 1900 to form the Labour Representation Committee which won 29 seats in the 1906 election (thereafter as the Labour Party). Leaving aside the Irish voters, for the English what had been a two-party system of Liberals versus Conservatives was now a three-party system. Not only that; the new party was also socialist(ic) and promoted the interests of the "working class" – quite a threat to the establishment. It is interesting that none of the leading characters of the fledgling Labour Party at the time, i.e., Hardie, Henderson, and Macdonald, ever wanted the party to be called "socialist" and indeed to this day it never has been.

Given that the law as set out by Parliament in the Ballot Act of 1872 could be construed by any reasonable person as requiring winning candidates to gain an absolute majority of votes, something which in a two-way contest was not problematic, a three-way contest in every constituency after the Redistribution legislation of 1885 introduced single-member constituencies throughout the entire country could result in no candidate winning a majority of votes in many constituencies. The voting system would collapse. *Something had to be done.*

THE ROYAL COMMISSION & CONSPIRACY THEORY

A Royal Commission into systems of election was established in 1908 and reported in 1910 (the report CD5163, is an exhaustive, detailed, and diligent analysis of electoral systems across the world at that time). They rejected PR. They recommended AV, at least that way a winner with a real majority would emerge.

What was in the minds of the commissioners? Whatever it was, what they said in paragraph 4 of their report was shocking. In paragraphs 1 to 3 they briefly summarised the purpose of the Commission, the broad nature of electoral systems, and voting procedure. Paragraph 4 then begins with these words:

4. Election – **Successful candidates are determined by relative, not absolute majority, i.e., to secure election it is not necessary to obtain more than half the valid votes cast, but only more votes than any other candidate.** *The instructions in the Ballot Act on this point provide only (sec. 2) that ". . . . . the returning officer shall . . . . ascertain the result of the poll by counting the votes given to each candidate and shall forthwith declare to be elected the candidates or candidate to whom the majority of votes have* *been given . . . "; **but in the absence of any directions as to what is to be done in the event of no candidate receiving an absolute majority it must be assumed that relative majority is intended.***

This is a remarkable assumption, indeed shocking, and clearly unlawful, and with these words in bold text above in paragraph 4 of their report the commissioners usurped without lawful authority an important function of the judges – the interpretation of statute law. Writing paragraph 4 in their report the way they did tends to confirm that the Commissioners knew that the draftsman of the Ballot Act may either have erred in his choice of words or in his failure to elaborate or in fact intended the word "majority" to be applied with its natural meaning. Whatever was in the minds of the Commissioners, in 1872, when the Ballot Act became law, when the two-party binary choice prevailed, there was no issue with the meaning of the word "majority" and that is probably why the Ballot Act says nothing about it. It meant more than half then and it means more than half now.

This is the reason *that the United Kingdom uses a first past-the-post system of winning candidate selection in general elections. We do not use it because the law requires us to. We use it because the Royal Commissioners unlawfully engineered it that way in 1910 to favour the political party that represented the interests of the Establishment – the Conservative Party.*

The commissioners declined to recommend PR, preferring instead to preserve the single-member constituencies system which had the support of most members of the House of

Commons at that time, but they recommended a system (AV) which they knew full well had no support in the Conservative-dominated House of Lords and would never pass into law. The Conservatives feared that under the AV ranking system, voters who supported the progressive parties, i.e., Liberals and Labour, would rank them first and second, thus squeezing out the Conservatives in most constituencies.

In the new Edwardian political landscape, if in three-way contests the progressive vote would now be split between the Liberals and the new Labour Party, a relative majority system would optimise the likelihood of the Conservative Party winning elections. Was this a factor in the Commissioners' thinking, and could it be the reason why they inserted paragraph 4 into their report, attempting to legislate unconstitutionally and without lawful authority?

IS FIRST PAST THE POST LEGITIMATE?

This is a rather big question, but the answer is no. Let us look at what the law says and how it has been and is being applied. In the Ballot Act of 1872, lawyers of the Civil Service wrote that winning candidate(s) in general elections would be "the candidates or candidate to whom the majority of votes have been given". These words were written at a time when Victorian Britain was a de facto two-party state and voter choices were binary between Liberal and Conservative candidates. In 1885, the Redistribution Act introduced single member constituencies throughout the United Kingdom. In every constituency, in a two-party system, the winning candidate would receive more than half of the votes and the losing candidate less than half. We know that the new Labour Party won 29 seats in the general election of 1906 and transformed the country into a multi-party state. We also know that the letter of the law required candidates to win a "majority of votes" to be elected but that this would be potentially impossible in many constituencies thereafter. We also know that the response of the authorities to these set of unplanned circumstances was to recognise that *something had to be done.*

We know that the response was to establish a Royal Commission to look at voting systems around the world. We know that the Royal Commission recommended a system, the Alternative Vote, where voters rank the candidates instead of just choosing one, but we know also that the Commissioners were well aware that there was no support for AV in the House of Lords and that it would never pass into law. We also know that the Commissioners did something ultra vires and usurped the judiciary's role and set out their own interpretation of statute law (in the Ballot Act). We also know that when the wording in the Ballot Act was transferred into the Representation of the People Act of 1918 the singular version "candidate to whom the majority of votes have been given" remained unaltered. What we do not know is why Parliament did not specify unequivocally what they meant. Yet, we know that Royal Commissioners had already filled the gap – without any lawful authority.

Based on the analysis set out in this book, there seems to be little doubt that the selection of winning candidates by "relative majority" based as it was on an unlawful proposition in 1910, and a blatant usurpation of a function of the judges, is a fraud. This is a fortiori so as Parliament and successive Executives throughout the 20th century have had ample opportunities to qualify the word "majority" in several iterations of the Representation of the People Acts but have never done so. One wonders why not.

All, then, that we are left with in support of the current system, is an unlawful act.

HUMAN RIGHTS AND FIRST PAST THE POST

Does the First Past the Post system of voting infringe the human rights of citizens of the United Kingdom? To answer this question, which will be answered in the affirmative, let us start with the statutory context, i.e., what is written in the Law. After that, we shall embark upon a short historical journey describing the origins of the European Court of Human Rights and the significance or otherwise of leading cases. The question will be asked – what practical impact has the European Court of Human Rights had on the citizens of the United Kingdom? The suggestion will be offered that the answer is – none. The author will challenge the relevance of the European Court of Human Rights and how it can justify its annual budget of 500 million Euros. During this narrative, the author will endeavour to make the tale as interesting as possible. It is remarkably interesting.

The Statutory Context

Firstly, the context is the European Convention on Human Rights and our own Human Rights Act 1998. Broadly speaking, our statute is more or less the same as the ECHR. There is some irony here, given that the articles of the Convention were drafted in the middle of the twentieth century mainly by British lawyers. The determining article is Article 3 of the First Protocol, Right to Free Elections, which reads as follows:

"The High Contracting Parties undertake to hold free elections at reasonable intervals by secret ballot, under conditions which will ensure the free expression of the opinion of the people in the choice of the legislature".

The High Contracting Parties are the signatory states (the 47 members of the Council of Europe, which include Russia, Turkey, and Ukraine) and initially it was thought that the article placed obligations on the signatory states but did not confer any human rights on individuals. However, as the jurisprudence of the Convention evolved, European judges took a different view, and decided that human rights attaching to individuals could be inferred. Two in fact. First, the active right to vote, and second, the passive right to stand for election. As we saw earlier, voting is not a privilege conferred on citizens by their governments – it is a human right.

This remained the legal status of Article 3 for fifty years. Importantly, the final ten words of the article *"opinion of the people in the choice of the legislature"* remained subject to only the strictest of interpretations by the judges during that time. What could the words really mean? Why are they in the statute? Are they just semantic adornments? What did the draftsman intend?

No-one knew. Until 2015. In that year, the judges heard an application against the Bulgarian state. At the conclusion of the case, in their judgement, the judges made a statement that ran contrary to almost everything they had previously said about electoral systems in relation to Article 3 of the First Protocol. We shall return to this important story when the leading cases are being reviewed.

A Short Historical Journey

At the same time as the European Broadcasting Union was being founded in 1950, the Treaty of Paris was signed. This treaty founded the European Coal and Steel Community. The founding nations were those on whose soil most of the battles of WW2 had occurred on mainland Europe: Belgium, the Netherlands, Luxembourg, France, Germany, and Italy. In 1957, the Treaty of Rome was signed and with it arrived the EEC – the European Economic Community. Another milestone was reached on January 1st, 1973, when Ireland, Denmark, and the UK joined the EEC. In 1993, the European Single Market was established signalling four fundamental and inviolable freedoms – freedom of goods, services, people, and capital. And so, the politicians in Berlin and Paris, and elsewhere, dropped the word "economic" from the great European construct that they were creating, and it simply became the European Union. Ever-closer political union was the goal, and soon there would be the remarkable introduction in most of the European states of a single currency, the Euro. The EU quickly borrowed a flag and an anthem from another European institution that had been founded just before the Treaty of Paris, in 1949. "In 1983 the European Parliament in turn adopted the flag devised by the Council of Europe and recommended that it become the European Communities' emblem. The European Council gave its approval in June 1985. The European Union's institutions began to use the flag in 1986. The European flag has since become synonymous with a shared political project which unites all Europeans, transcending their diversity".

The Council of Europe and the European Court of Human Rights

The same group of leading European statesmen and thinkers who helped found the European Coal and Steel Community in 1950 and the European Economic Community in 1957 also founded in 1949 the Council of Europe. Their historic achievements were truly of colossal importance for the future peace and prosperity of what they were determined would be a united Europe. Among them were the Prime Minister of the United Kingdom Winston Churchill, the Chancellor and Minister for Foreign Affairs of the Federal Republic of Germany Konrad Adenauer, the Minister for Foreign Affairs of the French Republic Robert Schuman, the Prime Minister and Foreign Minister of Belgium Paul-Henri Spaak, the Prime Minister of the Republic of Italy Alcide de Gasperi, and the Secretary of State for Foreign Affairs of the United Kingdom, Ernest Bevin.

The Council of Europe was founded on three fundamental and inviolate principles: Human Rights, Democracy, and the Rule of Law. It has 47 member states, 27 of whom are members of the European Union. Its main institution is the European Court of Human Rights, founded in 1959 and based in Strasbourg. The purpose of the Court was and is to uphold the principles and articles of the European Convention on Human Rights, and to secure to everyone within the jurisdiction of the Court the rights and freedoms defined therein. Article 1 describes the obligation to respect human rights. Article 2 defines the right to life. Article 3 defines the prohibition of torture. Article 4 describes the prohibition of slavery. Article 5 sets out the right to liberty and security. Article 6 describes the right to a fair trial. Article 7 defines no punishment without law. Article 8 describes the right to respect for private and family life. Article 9 defines freedom of thought, conscience, and religion. Article 10 describes freedom of expression. Article 11 describes freedom of assembly and association. Article 12 protects the right to marry. Article 13 guarantees the right to an effective remedy. Article 14 prohibits discrimination. Article 15 allows states to derogate in times of war or other national emergency subject to strict conditions. Article 16 permits restrictions on the political activity of aliens. Article 17 prohibits the abuse of rights within the Convention. Article 18 sets out limitations on the restrictions of rights set out in the Convention.

The European Court of Human Rights is described by the Council of Europe in this way:

It is the permanent judicial body which guarantees for all Europeans the rights safeguarded by the European Convention on Human Rights. It is open to states and individuals regardless of nationality. The 47 member states of the Council of Europe are parties to the Convention.

There have been in excess of 10,000 judgements of the Court that have been ignored by the state complained against, the majority of these cases being against Italy, Russia, Ukraine, and Turkey. The United Kingdom has also ignored judgements of the Court that ruled against it. In 2009, the backlog of cases waiting to be heard numbered 120,000 which it was estimated would require forty-six years to hear and decide upon. The caseload expanded after the fall of the Soviet Union, and in 2011 the number of pending applications numbered in excess of 150,000. In such impossible circumstances, it is difficult to see how the Court could be said to be fulfilling its mission to guarantee the rights safeguarded by the Convention. Cases with merit brought before it were simply not being heard. However, such exigencies require drastic remedies, and the Court developed a strategy to rid itself of the backlog of cases – by ruling them as inadmissible. To achieve this, the Court created a novel procedure – empowering the judges to sit in "single-judge formations" in order to facilitate the rejection of the backlog of cases as inadmissible.

The Margin of Appreciation

As will be shown later, there is always a tension between politics and law, especially when their purposes and objectives are seemingly incompatible. The jurisprudence of the European Court of Human Rights includes a principle of law called the Margin of Appreciation. It is important to say something about this principle. It is called a principle of law, but it is respectfully submitted that it is nothing of the kind. It is a principle of politics, or where law and politics intersect irreconcilably, and something has to give. It is convenient to describe the Margin of Appreciation in the context of its application to Article 3 of the First Protocol as that is the subject-matter with which we are concerned. However, let us begin with general principles before proceeding to discuss how the Margin of Appreciation has been applied.

On the face of it, there is a reasonable rationale in support of the Margin of Appreciation. It is the "space for manoeuvre" granted to the executive branches of the member states in deciding difficult cases. The following text from the Council of Europe is highly apposite and worth setting out here:

"Given the diverse cultural and legal traditions embraced by each member state, it was difficult to identify uniform European standards of human rights. The Convention was envisaged as the lowest common denominator. While the issue of deference to the sovereignty of each member state continues to be raised, the enforcement of the Strasbourg organs' undertaking ultimately depends on the good faith and continuing cooperation of the member states. Consequently, the process of realising a "uniform standard" of human rights, protection must be gradual because the entire legal framework rests on the fragile foundations of the consent of the member states. The Margin of Appreciation gives the flexibility needed to avoid damaging confrontations between the Court and the member states and enables the Court to balance the sovereignty of member states with their obligations under the Convention".

Jurists and academics have not hesitated to condemn this political pragmatism, suggesting that it "undermines the universal nature of human rights". Given that the whole edifice rests on "the fragile foundations of the consent of the member states", it is difficult to disagree with them.

The Application of the Margin of Appreciation

In looking at how the judges have applied the Margin of Appreciation, the following words from the Council of Europe are of considerable significance:

"The way in which the Margin of Appreciation is applied is of great relevance, given that the Convention was created not in the interests of the states, but for the benefit of their citizens".

Five cases will be discussed; four of them are concerned with Article 3 of the First Protocol, Right to Free Elections, and one with Article 14 Prohibition of Discrimination (but where the electoral system was at the heart of the case). For the sake of convenience, the cases will be discussed in chronological order. Four of the cases are leading cases. The five cases are:

Liberal Party v United Kingdom 1980

Mathieu-Mohin & Clerfayt v Belgium 1988

Hirst v United Kingdom 2005

Riza and Others v Bulgaria 2015

Conner v United Kingdom 2019

Liberal Party v United Kingdom 1980

If anyone had good reason to resent the system of voting used in general elections in the United Kingdom, it was the Liberal Party. In general election after general election in the 20th century the party received enough votes to justify a significant number of elected MPs, but this never happened. The party came second in many constituencies, but under the first past-the-post system these votes are ignored. When the total number of votes for the party across the nation was divided by the small number of elected Liberal Party MPs it was usually the case that 400,000 votes were required to elect a Liberal Party MP. This contrasted with around 40,000 to elect a Conservative MP and 43,000 to elect a Labour MP. Liberal Party HQ decided to make an Article 14 discrimination application arguing that the grossly unfair electoral system discriminated against them

(It was indeed party HQ. The leader of the party at that time was David Steel (Lord Aikwood), and he has told the author that he himself had nothing to do with the case and cannot even remember it).

The ruling of the Court came on December 18th, 1980, and began with the following short summary paragraphs:

Article 25 of the Convention :

a) *A political party, as a gathering of people with a common interest, can be considered as a non-governmental organisation or a group of individuals.*

b) *Can a political party, as such, be considered as a victim of a violation of Article 3 of the First Protocol? (Question not pursued).*

Article 3 of the First Protocol : *Both simple majority system and the proportional representation system are compatible with this provision.*

Article 14 of the Convention in conjunction with Article 3 of the First Protocol:

One cannot derive from the combination of these provisions the right that all votes have an equal weight. Reference to the traditional majority system.

The judges' analyses of the Liberal Party submissions were uncompromising. Yes, the voting system did indeed discriminate against them and yes indeed the justification for retaining it was nakedly the partisan interests of the Conservative and Labour Parties. The judges went on to say:

"Article 14 of the Convention read in conjunction with Article 3 of the First Protocol protects every voter against discrimination directed at him as a person for the grounds mentioned in Article 14. This is not the same as a protection of equal voting influence for all voters. The question whether or not equality exists in this respect is due to the electoral system being applied. Article 3 of the First Protocol is careful not to bind the states as to the electoral system and does not add any requirement of 'equality' to the 'secret ballot'".

The judges then went on to defend the "simple majority system" that the United Kingdom does not use, and said:

"The simple majority system is one of the two basic electoral systems. It is or has been used in many democratic countries. It has always been accepted as allowing for the 'free expression of the opinion of the people', even if it operates to the detriment of small parties".

The application was therefore "manifestly ill-founded". There seems to be no doubt that judicial reasoning in this case is a model of how to apply the Margin of Appreciation in the interests of the states but not for the benefit of their citizens.

Mathieu-Mohin & Clerfayt v Belgium 1988

This was the first application to the Court brought solely under Article 3 of the First Protocol, Right to Free Elections. The fact-situation in the case is complex, and concerns internal

Belgian electoral and civil administration, and need not concern us. However, the judges availed themselves of the opportunity to flex their political muscles when applying the Margin of Appreciation to the interpretation of Article 3 of the First Protocol (hereafter P1-3). As far as the rights expressed in P1-3 are concerned, the Court said:

"The rights in question are not absolute. Since Article 3 (P1-3) recognises them without setting them forth in express terms, let alone defining them, there is room for implied limitations" (yes indeed - and by applying the same logic, there is also room for the converse - implied expansionary interpretation, author note).

Then, in discussing conditions Contracting States may subject the rights under P1-3 to, the Court said:

"It (the Court) has to satisfy itself that the conditions do not curtail the rights in question to such an extent as to impair their very essence and deprive them of their effectiveness . . . . in particular such conditions must not thwart the *free expression of the opinion of the people in the choice of the legislature*".

The Court went on to offer a suggestion about what electoral systems should really do:

"Reflect fairly faithfully the opinions of the people, and channel currents of thought so as to promote the emergence of a sufficiently clear and coherent political will".

How this is to be achieved when the system employed can result in three-quarters of the votes cast by the people being discarded to the waste bin and ignored could not have been a factor in the judges' thinking at that time. This was, however, another example of how to apply the Margin of Appreciation in the interests of the states but not for the benefit of their citizens.

The judges concluded that based on the infallibility of their rationale "no electoral system can eliminate wasted votes" (Proportional systems can, author note). The Court did not consider how many wasted votes were acceptable, nor what percentage of votes cast in the election that were wasted if exceeded would trigger a change in judicial thinking.

Hirst v United Kingdom 2005

John Hirst was at the time of his application to the Court serving a sentence for manslaughter in a British prison. As such, his situation was caught by Section 3 of the Representation of the People Act 1983 which prohibits prisoners from voting while incarcerated. The human right to vote, as a component of universal suffrage was protected by Article 3 of the First Protocol of the Convention. Mr. Hirst asked the High Court to intervene, but his application was dismissed.

Consequently, as all internal domestic remedies were exhausted, Mr. Hirst lodged an application to the European Court of Human Rights. The judges ruled unanimously that Mr. Hirst's human rights had indeed been violated, vis-à-vis Article 3 of the First Protocol and its underlying principle of universal suffrage.

The British Government repeatedly indicated that there would be no repeal of Section 3 of the Representation of the People Act and that prisoners will not be allowed to vote in general and municipal elections. While a human right under Article 3 of the First Protocol is being infringed, there was no suggestion that other human rights would be denied to serving prisoners, such as under Article 3 Prohibition of Torture and inhuman or degrading treatment or punishment, or under Article 9 Freedom of Thought, Conscience, and Religion. Just the right to vote.

What about the Margin of Appreciation so diligently applied in the Liberal Party case and the Mathieu-Mohin case in favour of the member states? Prime Minister David Cameron complained that the position of the Court was distorting and discrediting the principles of fundamental human rights and that the Court was failing to apply the Margin of Appreciation fairly.

The Court responded with an eloquent summary of why the United Kingdom was in breach of its obligations under the Convention. It would appear that the voting rights of prisoners was something to preserve, protect, and defend against the member states, but grotesquely unfair electoral systems where millions of votes were discarded and ignored were not. In fairness, the Court's rationale was well argued – prisoners indeed should be allowed to vote as it is their human right, whereas the jurisprudence of the Court had not yet evolved to a point where it could spell out clearly exactly what rights were protected under Article

3 of the First Protocol. This maturity would come later in the case of Riza and Others v Bulgaria 2015.

Riza and Others v Bulgaria 2015

In this case, European judges finally announced to the signatory states and the world what the ten words "Opinion of the people in the choice of the legislature" really meant. Up till then, they had been subject to the strictest of interpretations. They used these dramatic words:

*"The active electoral right as guaranteed by Article 3 of Protocol No. 1 is not confined exclusively to the acts of choosing one's favourite candidates in the secrecy of the polling booth and slipping one's ballot paper into the box. **It also involves each voter being able to see his or her vote influencing the make-up of the legislature,** subject to compliance with the rules laid down in electoral legislation. To allow the contrary would be tantamount to rendering the right to vote, the election, and ultimately the democratic system itself meaningless".*

The subordinate clause *"subject to compliance with the rules laid down in electoral legislation"* is not problematic, i.e., there are circumstances in which this human right will not be available to everyone. For example, electoral systems have rules such as thresholds, usually set at 5%, and if you vote for a candidate who fails to meet the threshold, the candidate loses their deposit, and your vote is wasted.

In the Riza case, the judges used clear words. There can be no doubt that their words were intended to mean that electoral systems must be representative and that all votes must contribute to the composition of the legislature. In other words, the representation of the people in the legislature must be broadly in proportion to the votes cast by them. First Past the Post fails this test – by a country mile. The judgement in the Riza case was issued by the Court on the 13th of October 2015. Almost exactly four months earlier, a general election in the United Kingdom was held on 7th May. When the Court gave its judgement in the Riza case, the judges were aware of the grotesque outcome of that general election. As mentioned earlier, three quarters of the votes of those who voted were discarded to the waste bin and ignored – 22 million votes. Were the judges alarmed that a leading member of the Council of Europe and at the time a leading state of the European Union with all that that implies for the rights and freedoms of its citizens should be exhibiting the characteristics of a banana republic? Or worse? A fortiori, as the mainstream media such as the BBC, ITN, and Sky News passed not a single comment on it?

This being so, why was Conner v United Kingdom 2019 ruled inadmissible?

Conner v United Kingdom 2019

This application, submitted by the author, argued that the statement in the Riza case - "each voter being able to see his or her vote influencing the make-up of the legislature" was directly relevant to his situation and the doctrine of precedent should apply, i.e., the Court should apply Riza and find for t he applicant.

The applicant's submission summarised why he had not voted in a general election for 30 years because he lived in one of the "safest seats" in the country which was continuously held by an MP of a party that the applicant did not support. If he voted, his vote would be ignored, and voting under such circumstances was pointless.

In this case, a judge with strong ties to the United Kingdom and the University of Nottingham, sent these words to the applicant roughly two months after the application was submitted:

"The European Court of Human Rights, sitting on 11 July 2019 in a single-judge formation pursuant to Articles 24/2 and 27 of the Convention, has examined the application as submitted. The application refers to Article 3 of Protocol No. 1.

The Court finds that the applicant was not sufficiently affected by the alleged breach of the Convention or the Protocols thereto to claim to be the victim of a violation within the meaning of Article 34 of the Convention. Accordingly, these complaints are incompatible ratione personae with the provisions of the Convention within the meaning of Article 35/3/a.

The Court declares the application inadmissible".

Article 34 reads as follows:

The Court may receive applications from any person, non-governmental organisation or group of individuals claiming to be the victim of a violation by one of the High Contracting Parties of the rights set forth in the Convention or the Protocols thereto. The High Contracting Parties undertake not to hinder in any way the effective exercise of this right".

Article 35/3/a reads as follows:

"The Court shall declare inadmissible any individual application submitted under Article 34 if it considers that: the application is incompatible with the provisions of the Convention or the Protocols thereto, manifestly ill-founded, or an abuse of the right of individual application".

The judge did not follow the doctrine of precedent and apply Riza. It is submitted that he should have. However, again we see the political nature of the Margin of Appreciation manifest itself and we are left wondering: what is the point of the European Court of Human Rights?

Human Rights: Concluding Thoughts

It is widely accepted in virtually all jurisdictions that judges make policy decisions, and this is also true of the judges of the European Court of Human Rights. Yet, what else can they do? It is well-known that judges in the highest courts sit as instruments of state authority and policy decisions are frequently forced upon them. In so far as the status of the representative nature of electoral systems within the signatory states is concerned, it seems that the judges open themselves up to the criticism that many of their judgements are not legal, but political. So much political elasticity has been applied to the implementation of the Margin of Appreciation that it may well be at breaking point. We should remind ourselves that the Convention exists not to shore up the politics of the 47 signatory states but for the benefit of its citizens. These words from the Commissioner of Human Rights at the Council of Europe are helpful in understanding the frustration that is being experienced at the intersection of politics and law:

"Our work is based on co-operation and good faith. When you don't have that, it is very difficult to have an impact. We lack the tools to help countries that don't want to be helped".

It is a sad and rather defeatist perspective, or perhaps an appeal to the states that a budget of 500 million Euros is not enough. Look at the thousands of cases they have to throw out and the reality that the European Court of Human Rights in fact has no enforcement powers.

Another major difficulty is that decisions of the Court are not binding on the governments of the signatory states. In the United Kingdom, The Supreme Court has accepted that they must be taken into consideration and has established a "Mirror Principle" which provides for UK citizens receiving "no less but no more" than citizens of other signatory states. However, politics matters. As we have seen, the court has ruled on more than one occasion that prisoners must be allowed to vote – it is their human right – but the government of the United Kingdom simply refuses to allow it. In 2017, the Russian Constitutional Court rejected the decision of the Court to compensate the former oil corporation Yukos in the sum of 1.87 billion Euros as in its view the judgement was not compatible with the Russian Constitution. This is one of over 1,500 judgements of the court that the Russian state has declined to comply with.

These political difficulties in enforcing judgements of the court are in sharp contrast with the jurisdiction of the Court of Justice of the European Union (CJEU, formerly ECJ). The supremacy of community law over the law of member states established in Costa v ENEL 1964 and grudgingly accepted by the judicial committee of the House of Lords in R v Secretary of State for Transport, ex parte Factortame (No 4) 1990 has never been seriously challenged.

Under scrutiny, the relationship between Law and Politics reveals a harsh reality. When push comes to shove, Law yields. Has anyone ever successfully served a writ on a tank? This does not mean however that the judgement in the Riza case in 2015 does not matter. It does, and our human right to a representative voting system for general elections is now enshrined in Human Rights Law.

Try telling that to the government of the United Kingdom, who are determined to prevent that right ever being successfully exercised.

GUIDE ON ARTICLE 3 OF PROTOCOL NO. 1 – ANOTHER CONSPIRACY THEORY

The Directorate of the Jurisconsult at the European Court of Human Rights in Strasbourg is responsible for, amongst other things, the preparation and maintenance of guides to the articles of the Convention. These guides are of considerable importance in that they set out principles of interpretation applied to the articles by the judges, and also describe the leading cases over time and the legal significance of the cases. The guides are of particular importance to lawyers, law students, and even the judges, as they set out in summary form what is important and so relieve the professionals and students from the laborious task of reading the actual case judgements themselves – which can be an onerous task as they are extremely long and invariably complex. The guide document for Article 3 of the First Protocol, Right to Free Elections, runs to 33 pages.

We can be quite sure that those administrative assistants tasked with the job of updating the guidelines are qualified lawyers – it would simply not be possible for even a para-legal to do the work. We can also be quite sure that the nature of the work and its output requires a highly professional regime of inspection and quality control – always searching for errors and omissions in the drafts of updates. The objective of course – to get it right.

In our discussion of the Margin of Appreciation and its application by the Court, we reviewed the importance of the case of Riza and Others v Bulgaria 2015. This case set out new judicial thinking with respect to the interpretation of Article 3 of the First Protocol – Right to Free Elections, to such an extent that there seemed to be operating a major shift in the evolution of the jurisprudence of the Court. A new milestone.

Let us restate what the judges said in the Riza case:

*"The active electoral right as guaranteed by Article 3 of Protocol No. 1 is not confined exclusively to the acts of choosing one's favourite candidates in the secrecy of the polling booth and slipping one's ballot paper into the box. **It also involves each voter being able to see his or her vote influencing the make-up of the legislature,** subject to compliance with the rules laid down in electoral legislation. To allow the contrary would be tantamount to rendering the right to vote, the election, and ultimately the democratic system itself meaningless".*

As we observed, the judges used clear words – noticeably clear indeed, and we observed that the United Kingdom's first past the post system of voting fails this test. However, when the lawyers at the Directorate updated the Guidelines to set out the significance of the Riza case, this is what they wrote at paragraph 10:

"However, the vote of each elector must have the possibility of affecting the composition of the legislature, otherwise the right to vote, the electoral process and, ultimately, the democratic order itself, would be devoid of substance (Riza and Others v Bulgaria, 2015, at 148)".

There is no doubt that put this way, first past the post *passes* this test. All that is required is to vote for the winning candidate and the voter does indeed affect the composition of the legislature – the *possibility* of doing so is present in the system.

But this is not what the judges said in the Riza case. They meant *certainty*, not possibility. They specifically referred to "each voter".

The question then arises - how could the lawyers get this so terribly wrong? This is a question that the author has no answer to, only his opinion. It is for the reader to decide if the author is splitting hairs or points to something sinister. It could be incompetence, but that seems unlikely. What do you think?

CONCLUSION

I have a vote - so I must be living in a democracy - right? All too often, journalists and politicians refer to "our parliamentary democracy" or "our democracy" and those who do not are so scarce that they are invisible. Some journalists are keen to point out that they are republicans yet would never dream of challenging the notion that the United Kingdom is a democracy. This book has issued such a challenge. It has been shown that the system of winning candidate selection by relative majority (first past the post) used in general elections for the Westminster parliament is a fraud, and moreover that it infringes the human rights of our citizens. It has been shown that the United Kingdom has not yet completed its long journey to democracy, but that its ancient political institutions and unwritten constitution in so far as they can remain unfettered by vested interests have every prospect of facilitating safe arrival at that destination. In this ancient society, things take time.

When the lawyers of the Civil Service during Gladstone's first administration inserted the words "majority of votes" into the Ballot Act of 1872, we are stuck with the unavoidable conclusion that in a binary political system they meant more than half (a fortiori, given the number of uncontested two-member constituencies at that time).

This is the ordinary meaning of the word "majority". It is not unreasonable therefore to suggest that, had they meant "largest number", i.e., relative majority, a nuanced variant, they would have said so explicitly. They were drafting a law of historic importance in the political and democratic evolution of the greatest power in the world at that time in the nineteenth century, and it seems highly unlikely that they were being negligent. The matter would have been picked up at peer review time and there would consequently be no ambiguity and no doubt. Yet, it seems that even though we shall never know, we do know that the Royal Commissioners in 1910 sensed the need to address the issue, and it has been shown how fraudulently they addressed it. We also know that in order to have a working majority in the House of Commons a political party needs more than half of the members – at least 326. This reminds us that in our political system the word "majority" has a natural meaning. Of course, we also know that in our system of voting, it does not have a natural meaning.

There are some other things that we know. We know that the Parliament of the United Kingdom is sometimes referred to as the "Mother of Parliaments". We know that the Civil Service in our nation is much admired throughout the developed world. We also know that the nation-state that is the United Kingdom of Great Britain and Northern Ireland has an ancient legislature. We also know what is required to be elected to this ancient legislature, and we know that the ancient legislature has proved incapable of specifying unequivocally how its composition is to be determined. It is in practice determined by relative majority, but the law simply states "majority", a word whose common meaning is more than half. We also know that this anomaly has not been corrected by politicians despite ample opportunities for over a century. However, there is almost certainly a good reason for this. Fear. Fear of being complicit in proposing legislation that would change the letter of the law as written into the Ballot Act in 1872 in Victorian Britain on a matter of such enormous national importance. On the other hand, we know that our sovereign Parliament can make or unmake any law that it chooses, and no Parliament can be bound by a predecessor nor bind a successor. Yet still the politicians do not seem willing to go there.

We also know that the supervision of the behaviour and performance of Returning Officers at general elections is the responsibility of the Electoral Commission. We would expect such a body to err on the side of caution.

Yet, the guidelines of the Electoral Commission vis-à-vis the behaviour of Acting Returning Officers in declaring winning candidates in the constituencies during general elections state this:

Announcement of the result *After consulting the candidates and agents and after any recount, the (A)RO will announce the* *votes cast for all candidates and* **declare the candidate with most votes** *as the candidate elected to be the MP for the constituency.*

Yet, we know that statute law does not support this. The Electoral Commission appears to be trying to out-do the Royal Commissioners of 1910 in how statute law should be interpreted. Fraudulently. Now, "majority of votes" has been translated into "most votes" by a quango. But this is ultra vires and unlawful.

We can also say with some certainty that in 1910 the Royal Commissioners who usurped the role of the judiciary had no more right to interpret British statute law than Emmeline Pankhurst or Kaiser Wilhelm II. Yet they did, and seem to have got away with an unlawful and scandalous act.

We have also seen that judges in the European Court of Human Rights seem to have changed their attitudes to the highly unsatisfactory doctrine of the Margin of Appreciation and concluded that in the 21st century there really has to be a limit to the number of wasted votes in general elections so that the Council of Europe's founding principle of representative democracy is upheld.

So, where does all this leave us? For over a century, the Labour and Conservative parties in the United Kingdom have most of the time done their utmost to retain the first past the post system. To their credit, the judges who ruled in the Liberal Party case in 1980 stated unequivocally that these two parties did this because it gave them an enormous electoral advantage that ensured a duopoly, that they knew this and did not try to hide it, and that their foremost consideration was not the interests of the nation that they were serving, but their own party interests. Indeed, it was common to hear senior members of the main parties arrogantly assert that voting for anyone else was a wasted vote. After all this time, there is little evidence that the two main parties have any intention of changing their positions. For them, it is Party before Country. Party before our people. Shame on them.

In a recent poll of the membership of the Labour Party, three-quarters of the members said that they wanted proportional representation to be adopted as party policy. This may be the only way to achieve electoral reform. Unfortunately, the Labour Party would need to win back Scotland to form a government, but this does not appear to be even a remote possibility, and the English will never vote for a Labour-SNP pact. In any case, at the time of writing, the leadership of the Labour Party are determined to preserve the current fraudulent system.

Referendums appear to be off the agenda forever, after the strategically disastrous and pointless AV referendum of 2011 ensured that there will never be another one for several generations. This is probably a good thing, as the British public are not interested in electoral reform. They have a vote, so they live in a democracy, right?

The defenders of the fraudulent first past the post system have argued that it is the most widely "used" system in the world, and this is the kind of lie that progressive thinkers and reformers are up against. The lie is based on a false notion, i.e., that voters "use" electoral systems, but of course they do not. They vote. It is nation-states who "use" electoral systems. The lie suggests that two billion people "use" first past the post when in fact only a small handful of countries of any size use the system. These countries are predominantly former colonies of the British Empire, the most populous being India, the United States, and Canada. Yet, the lie told often enough becomes the truth. The men who put out the lies will not be overcome anytime soon, but they will be overcome, as Lenin was wrong, and they themselves are on the wrong side of history. Yet, historians may not be their harshest judges. That role will probably fall to their children.

For those of us who would rid ourselves of the offensive first past the post system that brings shame on our country and makes us a laughingstock to our democratic neighbours on the European mainland, and beyond, let us not forget the distinction between symptoms and real problems. Our problem is not Brexit, political party sleaze, corruption, the selling of honours, or anything of that kind. These are symptoms. Our real problem is that we do not have a representative legislature. When we do, politicians will have to talk to each other, instead of engaging in puerile confrontations in a Dickensian Museum symbolising class-based two-party politics and vestiges of old hereditary rule – something that mature societies like France and America rid themselves of in the late eighteenth century. Let us also not forget that, lest we despair, in this ancient society, Things

Take Time (Put up in a place where it's easy to see, the cryptic admonishment TTT. When you feel how depressingly slowly you climb, its well to remember that – Things Take Time. Piet Hein, Grooks, Vol.1).

---------------------- **The End** ---------------------

AUTHOR PROFILE

Thomas Conner was born in Glasgow in 1951. He lives in Cornwall and is a retired chartered software engineer and academic lawyer. He studied history and politics at the University of Edinburgh, law at the University of London and the Open University and computer science at the British Computer Society. He started researching the legal status of the first past the post system in 2015 after the results in that election proved so grotesque. Apart from the Liberal Party in 1980, he is the only person to have challenged the first past the post system in the European Court of Human Rights.

Printed in Great Britain
by Amazon

20362648R00045